Fluõ | **Travel**

CÁDIZ

COLOR MAP

Cádiz Color Map
By Isaac M. Harland

First Edition: March 2019

Scale / 1:7500

| ■■■■■ 100m

| ■■■■■■■ 500ft

At a Glance

Country	Spain
Region	Andalusia
Native Name	Cádiz
Established	1104 BC
Language	Spanish
Currency	Euro (EUR)
Plug Type	C, F (230V)
Driving	Right-hand
Population	123948
Area	12.10 sq.kms
Postal Code	11071
Area Code	+(34)956
Timezone	CET (+1)
Timezone DST	CEST (+2)

Map   3

Map Overview

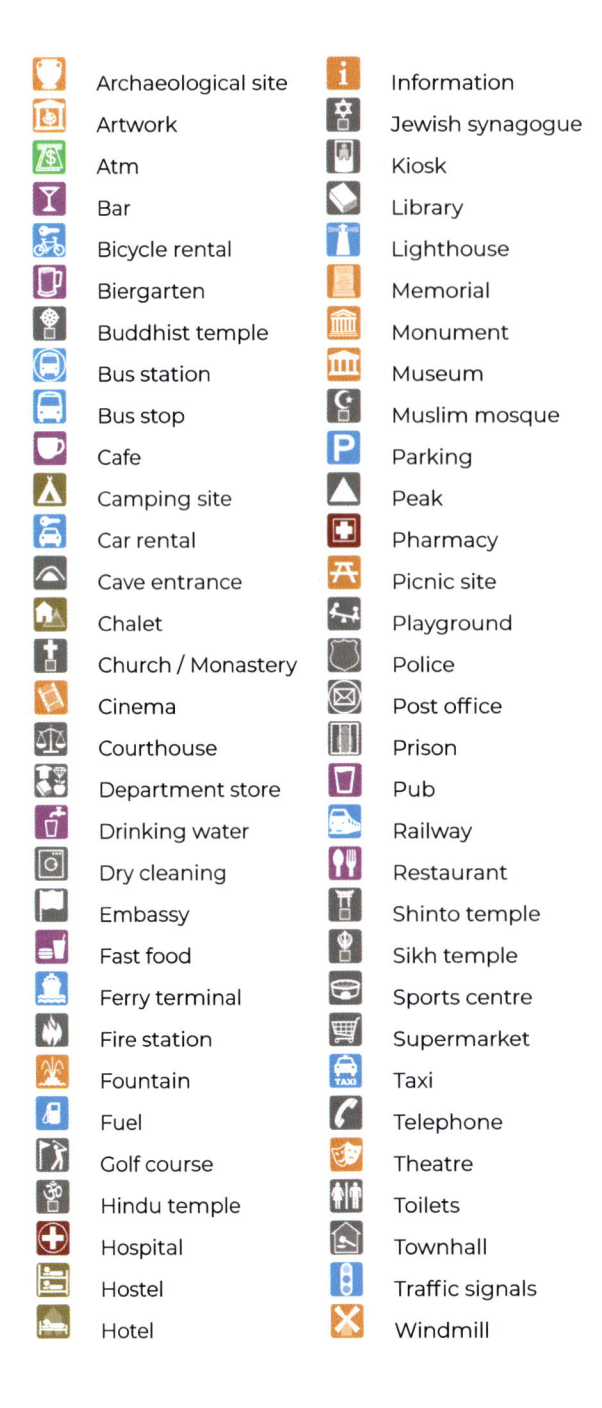

	Archaeological site		Information
	Artwork		Jewish synagogue
	Atm		Kiosk
	Bar		Library
	Bicycle rental		Lighthouse
	Biergarten		Memorial
	Buddhist temple		Monument
	Bus station		Museum
	Bus stop		Muslim mosque
	Cafe		Parking
	Camping site		Peak
	Car rental		Pharmacy
	Cave entrance		Picnic site
	Chalet		Playground
	Church / Monastery		Police
	Cinema		Post office
	Courthouse		Prison
	Department store		Pub
	Drinking water		Railway
	Dry cleaning		Restaurant
	Embassy		Shinto temple
	Fast food		Sikh temple
	Ferry terminal		Sports centre
	Fire station		Supermarket
	Fountain		Taxi
	Fuel		Telephone
	Golf course		Theatre
	Hindu temple		Toilets
	Hospital		Townhall
	Hostel		Traffic signals
	Hotel		Windmill

Paseo de
Santa Bárbara

Avenida Doctor Gómez Ulla

Calle Santa Rosalía

Antonio Burgos

Facultad
de Medicina

Plaza F

Aulario Simón
Bolívar

le Chile

8

Carlos III

Calle Gravina

Calle Bendición de Dios

Calle Vea Murguia

Baluarte de la Candelaria

Alameda de Apodaca

Calle Buenos Aires

Calle Ahumada

Calle Isabel la Católica

Plaza Argüelles

Calle Honduras

Calle Costa Rica

Aparcamiento de Autocaravanas

Avenida Nuevo Mundo

Mejico

Calle Veedor

Calle Antonio López

Plaza de Mina

Calle Zaragoza

Calle Cervantes

Calle San Pedro

Calle Ancha

Calle Sagasta

Plaza Viudas

Calle Soledad

Calle Virgili

Calle Torre

Calle San José

Calle Beato Diego

Calle Rosa

Plaza de España

Plaza de España

Diputación Provincial de Cádiz

Terminal Transmediterranea Canarias

9

5

Castillo
de Santa
Catalina

Castillo de San
Sebastián

Castillo
de San
Sebastián

Castillo
de San
Sebastián

Paseo Fernando Quiñones

Playa de
La Caleta

Playa de
La Caleta

Baluarte
de los Mártires

Avenida Duque de Nájera

Calle Ma

Calle San

Calle Enca

Calle Rosa

Calle Patrocinio

Calle Vidal

Plaza de
la Reina

Calle de La Pal

Calle Ángel

Calle Paraguay

Calle San Félix

Calle Lubet

Calle Venezuel

Calle Campo del S

de

Dragados
Off-shore

Puente de la Constitución de 1812

Puente de la Constitución de 1812

Fuerte de San Luis

Bajo de las Cabezuelas

Manuel Echevarr

Avenida Esteban Meinadier

Avenida Esteban Meinadier

15

Puente de la Constitución de 1812

Castillo de Matagorda

Playa de
la Ministra

Calle Br

Calle Perú

Calle Argentina

Calle Arg

Manuel Echevarria

Viaducto del Río San Pedro

Calle Ecuador

el Echevarria

Avenida Esteban Meinadier

Calle Proa

Avenida Fermín Salvoc

Polígono
Industrial
de las Cabezuelas

Avenida Esteban Meinadier

Chile

Ecuador

Mayor

Mesana

Call

Calle Colombia

Autovía de Acceso a

Calle Panamá

Calle Bolivia

16

P

9

13

Plaza de
Asdrúbal

Calle Amílcar Barca

Castillo
de Matagorda

Castillo
de San
Lorenzo
del Puntal

Puente José León de Carranza

18

Calle Ceuta

Paseo Marítimo

14
Plaza
San Juan
de Puerto
Rico

Plaza de
la Zona
Franca

Calle de la Adelfa

Calle Retama

Calle Los Barrios

Calle Algeciras

Calle La Línea de La Concepción

Ronda de Vigilancia de la Zona Franca

Calle Gibraltar

Paseo Marítimo

TAXI

Calle de Nelson Mandela

Avenida José León de Carran

Castillo
de Cortadura

Muralla
de Cortadura

Instituto
de Cortadura

Algeciras

Algodona

Calle Puerto de Santa Mi

19

18

Altadis

Avenida José León de Carranza

Puente José León de Carranza

Puente José León de Car...

. Puerto Real

...godonales

15

20

Playa de
la Cortadura

Carretera de Andalucía

Carretera de Andalucía